ENGLISH
TIME
STUDENT BOOK
4

Susan Rivers
Setsuko Toyama

OXFORD
UNIVERSITY PRESS

198 Madison Avenue
New York, NY 10016 USA

Great Clarendon Street
Oxford OX2 6DP England

Oxford New York
Auckland Cape Town Dar es Salaam Hong Kong Karachi
Kuala Lumpur Madrid Melbourne Mexico City Nairobi
New Delhi Shanghai Taipei Toronto

With offices in

Argentina Austria Brazil Chile Czech Republic France Greece
Guatemala Hungary Italy Japan South Korea Poland Portugal
Singapore Switzerland Thailand Turkey Ukraine Vietnam

ISBN-13: 978 0 19 436419 5
ISBN-10: 0 19 436419 4

Library of Congress Cataloging-in-Publication Data
Rivers, Susan.
English time. Student book 4 / Susan Rivers, Setsuko Toyama.
p. cm.
Summary: Teaches English as a second language to beginning ESL students through the use of pictures, simple stories, and songs. Includes comprehension questions, vocabulary, and review.
ISBN-13: 978 0 19 436419 5
ISBN-10: 0 19 436419 4
1. English language--Textbooks for foreign speakers—Juvenile literature. [1. English language—Textbooks for foreign speakers.] I. Toyama, Setsuko. II. Title.
PE1128 .R487 2002
428.2'4'078--dc21 2002072268

Editorial Manager: Nancy Leonhardt
Editor: Paul Phillips
Associate Editors: Michael Cahill, Sarah Wales McGrath
Senior Production Editor: Joseph McGasko
Senior Designer: Maj-Britt Hagsted
Art Buyer: Elizabeth Blomster
Production Manager: Shanta Persaud
Production Coordinator: Eve Wong

Printing (last digit): 10 9 8

Printed in Hong Kong

Musical arrangements and chant music: William Hirtz

Illustrations: Lynn Adams/Evelyne Johnson Associates, Yvette Banek, Shirley Beckes/Craven Design, Randy Chewning/HK Portfolio, Inc., Bill Colrus, Mena Dolobowsky, Ruth J. Flanigan, Patrick Girouard, Margeaux Lucas/HK Portfolio, Inc., Susan Miller, John Nez, Vilma Ortiz-Dillon, Dana Regan, Michael Reid/HK Portfolio, Inc., Andrew Shiff, Jim Talbot

Original characters developed by Amy Wummer

"Digger's World" by Jim Talbot

Cover Illustrations: Jim Talbot

Cover Design: Silver Editions

Acknowledgement:
My hearty thanks go to Lesley Koustaff, Michael Cahill, OUP Tokyo, Shoko, Eiko, Hiromi, Nobuko, and Lori.—Setsuko Toyama

Table of Contents

Syllabus

Unit	Topic	Conversation Time	Word Time	Practice Time	Phonics Time
1	Camping Activities	Wake up, Annie! What time is it, Penny? It's seven o'clock. It's time for breakfast. Good. I'm hungry. Smells good. What's for breakfast? We're having bacon and eggs. Yum! My favorite!	cook breakfast listen to stories laugh at jokes climb a mountain watch the sunrise play cards wash the pots and pans clean the tent	Did you cook breakfast? Yes, I did. No, I didn't. I played cards. (all pronouns)	**Consonant Blend Review**
2	Amusement Park Activities	It's so hot. I'm really thirsty. Me, too. Let's get some juice. What kind of juice do you want? Pineapple juice, please. Uh-oh! I don't have enough money. That's okay. It's my treat. Here you are. Thanks a lot.	drink soda pop eat cotton candy win a prize go on a ride see a show have lunch buy tickets take pictures	She bought tickets. She didn't eat cotton candy. (all pronouns)	**-ed /t/** bak**ed**, chopp**ed**, kiss**ed** **-ed /d/** call**ed**, clean**ed**, play**ed**
3	Chores	Let me help you, Mom. Thanks. Be careful. It's heavy. No problem. I'm strong. Yes, you are. Help! Watch out! Are you okay? I think so. But look at my skateboard.	make the bed feed the pets sweep the floor take out the garbage do the laundry hang up the clothes put away the groceries set the table	What did she do? She swept the floor. (all pronouns)	**-ed /id/** dust**ed**, greet**ed**, invit**ed**, plant**ed**, wait**ed**, weed**ed**
	Review of Units 1–3				
4	Activities in Town	Excuse me. I'm looking for the museum. Is it far? Not really. Walk two blocks. Turn right. It's on the left. Did you say turn right or turn left? Turn right. It's on the left. Thank you very much. You're welcome. Have fun!	see a movie rent a video ride the bus visit a friend buy a donut mail a letter get a haircut take a taxi	I'm/She's/We're going to ride the bus. I'm not/She isn't/We aren't going to take a taxi. (all pronouns)	**-le** beet**le**, bicyc**le**, bott**le**, pood**le**, pudd**le**, unc**le**
5	Food and Drinks	What are you eating? Fried rice. Try some. It's good. No, thanks. Come on. Just a little. Oh, all right. But not too much. Here you go. Hey! It's delicious! I told you so.	taco/tacos burrito/burritos french fry/french fries hot dog/hot dogs spaghetti curry iced tea lemonade	What are you going to have? I'm going to have a hot dog. What's he going to have? He's going to have some curry. What are they going to have? They're going to have some curry. (all pronouns)	**-er** blist**er**, butt**er**, dinn**er**, lobst**er**, moth**er**, tig**er**
6	Seasons and Seasonal Activities	What's your favorite subject? I like math. It's fun. Excuse me. Where's the library? Go straight. It's across from the music room. Thanks. Sure. Oh. It's time for art class. Great. That's my favorite.	spring summer fall winter plant flowers pick apples build a snowman go to the beach play in the leaves go skiing	I'll plant flowers in the spring. I won't go skiing. (all pronouns)	**al** f**al**l, t**al**k **au** l**au**ndry, s**au**cer **aw** cr**aw**l, dr**aw**
	Review of Units 4–6				

Unit	Topic	Conversation Time	Word Time	Practice Time	Phonics Time
7	Sea Animals	Which one do you want? Oh, I don't know. They're all cute. Well, it's time to go. Please make up your mind. Um, okay. I'll take this one. Are you sure? I'm positive. Great. Let's get it. Dad, the cashier is over here.	whale dolphin eel shark octopus crab big small fast slow	The whale is bigger than the dolphin.	**ar** barn farm yard **or** corn fork storm
8	Land Animals	Dad! Guess what! What? There's a monkey on the car! Quick! Shut the window. Look! There it is. Oh, it's cute. It's not cute. It's scary. Don't worry. It won't hurt you. Aw! It's going away.	elephant cheetah giraffe snake turtle chimpanzee tall short fat thin	Which one is the tallest? The giraffe is the tallest.	**ou** house mouse mouth **ow** brown gown town
9	Recreation	Oh! I missed the ball. We won! We won! Congratulations. Nice game. It was close. Yeah, it was. Do you want to play again? Sure. This time we'll win. We'll see.	play Ping-Pong play badminton snorkel go fishing go horseback riding go sailing in-line skate listen to music	What do you like to do? I like to listen to music. What does he like to do? He likes to listen to music. (all pronouns)	**oo** cook look wood **oo** broom moon noodle
	Review of Units 7–9				
10	Hobbies	Wow! What a cool kite! Thanks. I made it myself. You're kidding! No, it's true. I made it. Was it hard? No, it was easy. I'll show you. Great! What do we need? Paper and string. Let's get some.	collect stickers sing build a model take a nap read a comic book make a video paint cycle	We like singing, but we don't like building models. She likes singing, but she doesn't like building models. (all pronouns)	**er** clerk dessert **ir** bird shirt **ur** curry purse
11	Planets	Wow! Did you see all the planets and stars? Yeah! That was a great show. Ms. Apple, can we go to the snack bar? Can we go to the gift shop? No, kids. We don't have time. Aw. But I want to buy a gift for my dad. And I'm thirsty. Please, Ms. Apple. We'll hurry. Sorry, kids. We have to catch the bus.	Mercury Venus Earth Mars Jupiter Saturn Uranus Neptune Pluto	I want to see Mercury. Let me look. He wants to see Mercury. Let him look. (object pronouns)	**oi** boil oil point **oy** boy joy oyster
12	Occupations	You dance very well. Thanks. I love dancing. I don't dance very well. Sure you do. You're a good dancer. But I don't practice enough. Well, practice makes perfect. I have an idea. Let's practice together. That's a great idea. Thanks.	musician/play the violin engineer/build things vet/help animals computer programmer/program computers nurse/take care of people artist/draw	Why do you want to be a vet? Because I like helping animals. Why does she want to be a vet? Because she likes helping animals. (all pronouns)	**Vowel Blend Review**
	Review of Units 10–12				

Classroom Language

Listen and repeat.

Collect the homework, please.
Okay.

Pass out the paper, please.
Can I help?

Share a book with your classmate.
Let's use mine.

Ask your classmate a question about page 24.
What's he doing?
23
24
23
24

May I get a drink of water?
Not right now. In a minute.

Make a sentence with the word "night."
night
I practice the piano at night.

Who can tell me the answer?
___ you want tofu?
Yes, I ___.
I can.
Me, too.

Please repeat after me.
"He wants fruit."
He wants fruit.

Please memorize page 18.
That's easy.

Who wants to erase the board?
I do.

No gum in class. Please get rid of it.
Sorry.

Next class, you will have
a test on Unit 12.
Which unit?
Unit 12.

Do You Remember?

 Listen and point.

1.
Hi, I'm Ted Lee. She's Annie Day.
We go to school by bus.
Hi, I'm Digger.

2.
I'm wearing a red and blue dress. He's wearing a blue cap.
I have a camera and some film.

3.
We live in Sunnyville.
There's a river. There isn't any snow.

4.
She listens to music in the morning.
He plays video games in the morning.
I have a snack in the morning.

5.
On Saturday, I was at the museum.
I wasn't at the museum. I was at the movie theater.

6.
Were you at the movie theater?
No, I was at the museum.
See you in Unit 1!

1

At the Campsite

Conversation Time

A. Listen and repeat.

B. Listen and point to the speakers.

C. Role-play the conversation with a partner.

1.
Wake up, Annie!

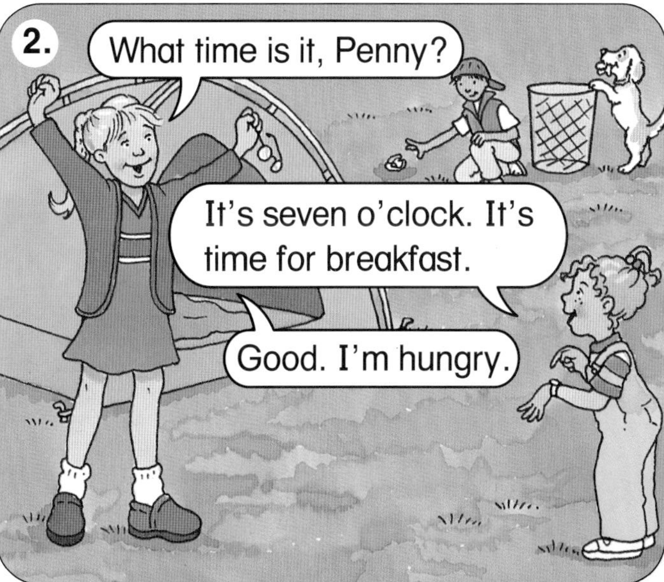
2.
What time is it, Penny?
It's seven o'clock. It's time for breakfast.
Good. I'm hungry.

3.
Smells good. What's for breakfast?
We're having bacon and eggs.

4.
Yum! My favorite!

D. Review. Listen and repeat.

What's wrong?

I can't find my sunscreen.

It's next to your camera.

Oh! There it is.

Word Time

A. Listen and repeat.

1. cook breakfast
2. listen to stories
3. laugh at jokes
4. climb a mountain
5. watch the sunrise
6. play cards
7. wash the pots and pans
8. clean the tent

B. Point and say the words.

C. Listen and point.

D. Write the words.
(See pages 63–66.)

5
4
8
1
7
6
3
2

Practice Time

A. Listen and repeat.

Did you cook breakfast?

Yes, I did.

No, I didn't. I played cards.

didn't = did not

cook	→	cooked	listen	→	listened	laugh	→	laughed	climb	→	climbed
watch	→	watched	play	→	played	wash	→	washed	clean	→	cleaned

B. Listen and repeat. Then practice with a partner.

1. he/wash the pots and pans?
   Yes

2. they/climb a mountain?
   No/watch the sunrise

3. she/clean the tent?
   Yes

4. you/listen to stories?
   No/climb a mountain

5. they/play cards?
   No/listen to stories

6. you/laugh at jokes?
   Yes

C. Look at page 2. Point to the picture and practice with a partner.

D. Listen and sing along. (See "Did Ted Watch the Sunrise?" on page 57.)

Phonics Time

A. Listen and repeat.

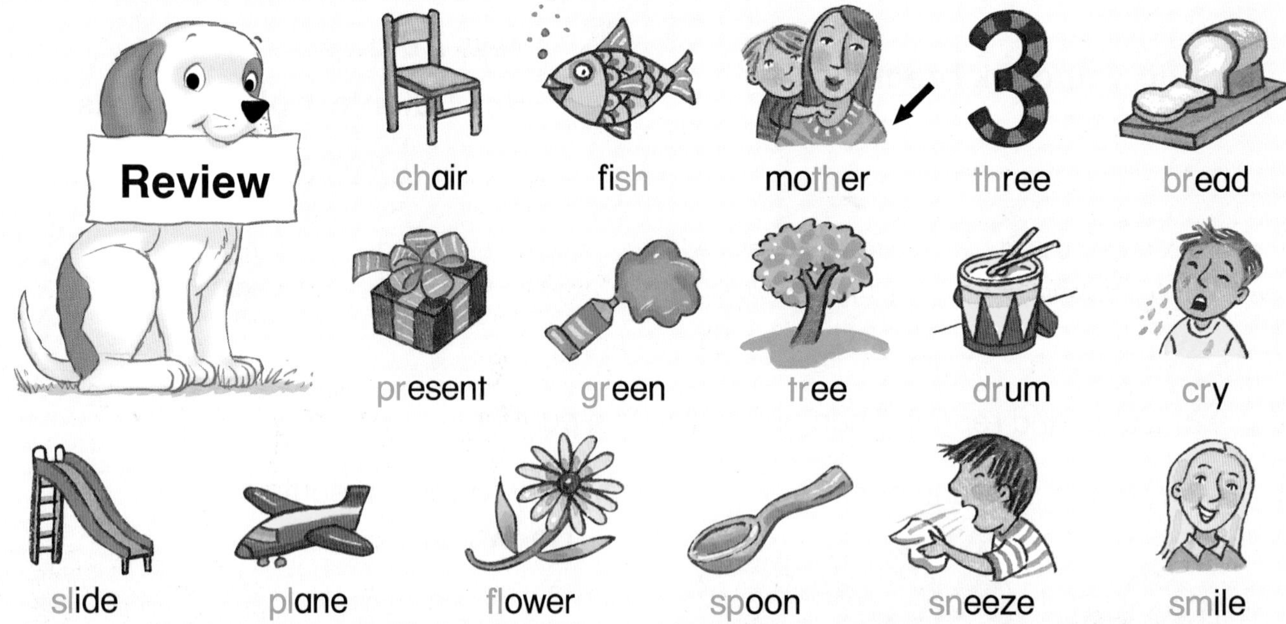
Review
chair
fish
mother
three
bread
present
green
tree
drum
cry
slide
plane
flower
spoon
sneeze
smile

B. Listen and write.

1. ____ing **2.** ____ell **3.** ____ay **4.** ____eep **5.** ____ain **6.** ____ree

C. Read the sentences. Write the numbers. Then listen.

1. Mother has a fish. She puts the fish on a dish.
2. Mother sees a tree. She sees three.
3. Mother is on a plane. The plane is over Spain.
4. Mother eats some cheese. Mother has to sneeze.

Madrid

2

At the Amusement Park

Conversation Time

A. Listen and repeat. **B.** Listen and point to the speakers.

C. Role-play the conversation with two other students.

1.
It's so hot. I'm really thirsty.
Me, too. Let's get some juice.

2.
JUICE
What kind of juice do you want?
Pineapple juice, please.

3.
Uh-oh! I don't have enough money.
That's okay. It's my treat.

4.
Here you are.
Thanks a lot.

D. Review. Listen and repeat.

Smells good. What's for lunch?

We're having pasta.

Yum! My favorite!

Here. Help yourself.

Word Time

A. Listen and repeat.

1. drink soda pop
2. eat cotton candy
3. win a prize
4. go on a ride
5. see a show
6. have lunch
7. buy tickets
8. take pictures

B. Point and say the words.

C. Listen and point.

D. Write the words.
(See pages 63–66.)

4

5

7

2

8

1

6

3

Practice Time

A. Listen and repeat.

She bought tickets. **She didn't eat cotton candy.**

drink	→	drank	eat	→	ate	win	→	won	go	→	went
see	→	saw	have	→	had	buy	→	bought	take	→	took

B. Listen and repeat. Then practice with a partner.

1. They / see a show
have lunch

2. She / take pictures
win a prize

3. We / have lunch
see a show

4. You / win a prize
take pictures

5. He / go on a ride
drink soda pop

6. I / drink soda pop
go on a ride

C. Look at page 6. Point to the picture and practice with a partner.

D. Listen and sing along. (See "Dan and Penny Saw a Show" on page 57.)

Phonics Time

A. Listen and repeat.

-ed
baked
chopped
kissed
-ed
called
cleaned
played

B. Do they both have the same **-ed** sound? Listen and circle ✔ or ✘.

1. washed
   talked
   ✔ ✘
2. climbed
   walked
   ✔ ✘
3. cooked
   studied
   ✔ ✘
4. listened
   played
   ✔ ✘

C. Read the sentences. Write the numbers. Then listen.

1. She brushed the cat and washed her dress.
2. She baked a pie and played some chess.
3. She chopped the logs and kissed the frog.
4. And then she called her mother.

3

Around the House

Conversation Time

A. Listen and repeat.

B. Listen and point to the speakers.

C. Role-play the conversation with a partner.

1.
Let me help you, Mom.
Thanks. Be careful. It's heavy.

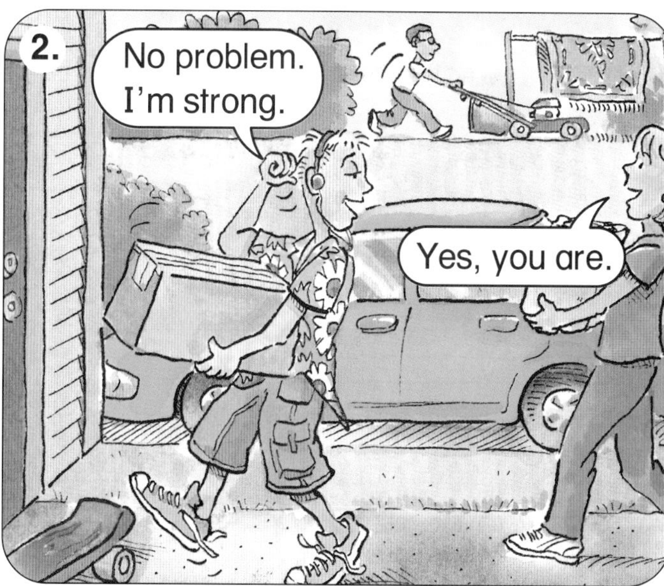
2.
No problem. I'm strong.
Yes, you are.

3.
Help!
Watch out!

4.
Are you okay?
I think so. But look at my skateboard.

D. Review. Listen and repeat.

What kind of juice do you want?

Orange juice, please. Uh-oh! I don't have enough money.

That's okay. It's my treat.

Word Time

A. Listen and repeat.

1. make the bed
2. feed the pets
3. sweep the floor
4. take out the garbage
5. do the laundry
6. hang up the clothes
7. put away the groceries
8. set the table

B. Point and say the words.

C. Listen and point.

D. Write the words.
(See pages 63–66.)

3
1
6
7
4
8
2
5

Practice Time

A. Listen and repeat.

What did she do? **She swept the floor.**

make → made	feed → fed	sweep → swept	take → took
do → did	hang → hung	put → put	set → set

B. Listen and repeat. Then practice with a partner.

1. she/do?
make the bed

2. he/do?
feed the pets

3. you/do?
put away the groceries

4. he/do?
do the laundry

5. they/do?
take out the garbage

6. you/do?
set the table

C. Look at page 10. Point to the picture and practice with a partner.

D. Listen and sing along. (See "What Did You Do?" on page 58.)

Phonics Time

A. Listen and repeat.

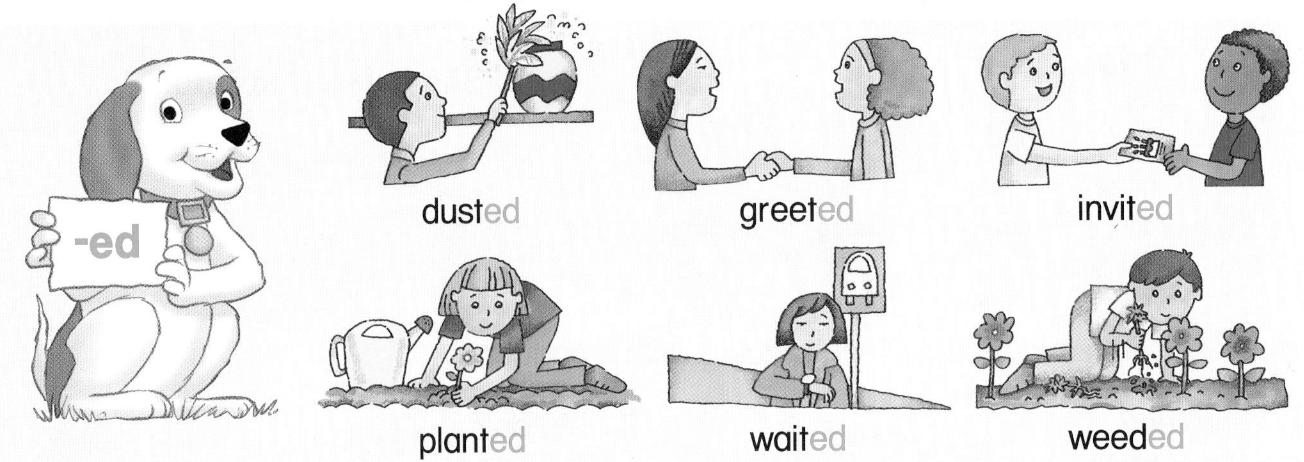

-ed
dusted
greeted
invited
planted
waited
weeded

B. Do they both end with the same sound? Listen and write ✔ or ✘.

1. painted / counted ☐
2. baked / roasted ☐
3. called / waited ☐
4. needed / folded ☐
5. weeded / dusted ☐

C. Read the sentences. Write the numbers. Then listen.

1. A bug wanted a home, so she planted a seed.
2. She waited and waited, and weeded and weeded.
3. Then she dusted, painted, and invited her sisters for lunch.
4. She greeted them with roasted beans.

Review 1

Digger's World

Story Time

A. Listen and repeat.

1.
Let me help you, Digger.
Thank you, Max. Be careful. It's heavy.

2.
No problem. I'm strong.
Yes, you are.
Did you cook breakfast?
Yes, I did.

3.
Good! I'm hungry. What's for breakfast?
We're having bacon and eggs.

4.
Watch out, Max!
Help!

5.
Are you okay, Max?
I think so. But look at the breakfast!

6.
Wake up, Max! It's time for breakfast!

B. Look at **A**. Listen and point.

C. Listen. Circle True or False.

1. True False **2.** True False **3.** True False **4.** True False **5.** True False

D. Role-play these scenes.

Activity Time

A. Read and find the picture. Then write the letter.

1. Eve waited for the bus. ____
2. Steve called his mother. ____
3. Kate smelled the flower and sneezed. ____
4. Brent baked a green cake. ____
5. Jeff kissed three fish. ____
6. Gail cleaned the plane. ____

a 

b 

c 

d 

e 

f 

B. What did they do? Listen and circle **a** or **b**.

1. a b 

2. a  b 

3. a b

4. a b 

5. a b 

6. a b 

C. Read the word. Then write the past form.

1. buy ____________	2. do ____________	3. drink ____________
4. eat ____________	5. feed ____________	6. go ____________
7. hang ____________	8. have ____________	9. make ____________
10. put ____________	11. see ____________	12. set ____________
13. sweep ____________	14. take ____________	15. win ____________

4

In Town

Conversation Time

A. Listen and repeat.

B. Listen and point to the speakers.

C. Role-play the conversation with a partner.

1.
Excuse me. I'm looking for the museum. Is it far?
Not really.
MAP

2.
Walk two blocks. Turn right. It's on the left.

3.
Did you say turn right or turn left?
Turn right. It's on the left.

4.
Thank you very much.
You're welcome. Have fun!

D. Review. Listen and repeat.

$2

 Watch out!

 Ouch!

 Are you okay?

 I think so. But look at the groceries!

Word Time

A. Listen and repeat.

1. see a movie
2. rent a video
3. ride the bus
4. visit a friend
5. buy a donut
6. mail a letter
7. get a haircut
8. take a taxi

B. Point and say the words.

C. Listen and point.

D. Write the words.
(See pages 63–66.)

7
3
4
5
1
2
8
6

Practice Time

A. Listen and repeat.

I'm **She's** **We're**	**going to ride the bus.**

I'm not **She isn't** **We aren't**	**going to take a taxi.**

B. Listen and repeat. Then practice with a partner.

1. She / mail a letter
   get a haircut

2. He / get a haircut
   mail a letter

3. We / see a movie
   rent a video

4. They / rent a video
   see a movie

5. You / buy a donut
   visit a friend

6. I / visit a friend
   buy a donut

C. Look at page 16. Point to the picture and practice with a partner.

D. Listen and sing along. (See "I'm Going to Rent a Video" on page 58.)

Phonics Time

A. Listen and repeat.

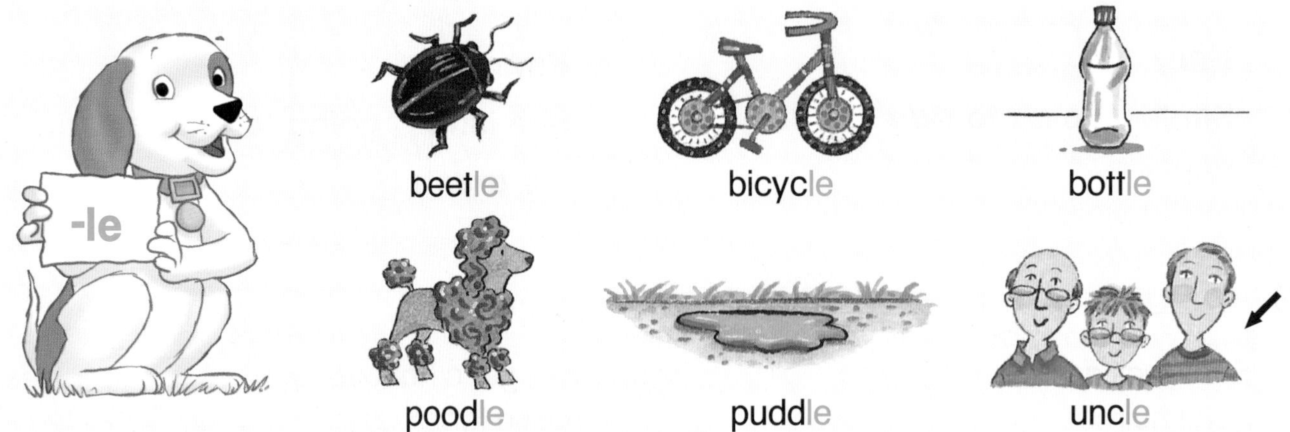
-le
beetle
bicycle
bottle
poodle
puddle
uncle

B. Listen and circle.

1.	2.	3.	4.	5.
popsicle	saddle	bottle	bicycle	puddle
middle	rattle	little	handle	riddle
uncle	beetle	candle	poodle	fiddle

C. Read the sentences. Write the numbers. Then listen.

1. The beetle is in the middle of a puddle.
2. Her uncle is on a bicycle.
3. He has a little poodle.
4. It's a poodle for the beetle in the middle of the puddle.

5

At the Food Festival

Conversation Time

A. Listen and repeat.

B. Listen and point to the speakers.

C. Role-play the conversation with a partner.

1.
What are you eating?
Fried rice. Try some. It's good.

2.
No, thanks.
Come on. Just a little.

3.
Oh, all right. But not too much.
Here you go.

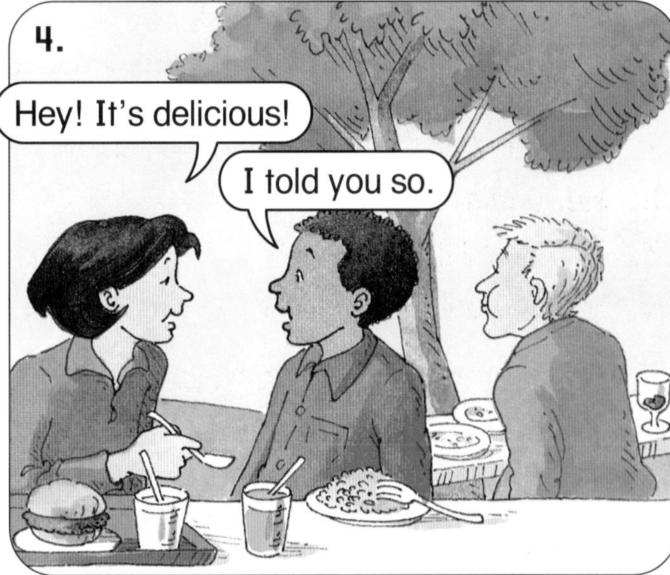
4.
Hey! It's delicious!
I told you so.

D. Review. Listen and repeat.

What did you buy?

I bought some donuts. Do you want one?

Yes, please. Thank you very much.

You're welcome.

Word Time

A. Listen and repeat.

1. taco/tacos

2. burrito/burritos

3. french fry/french fries

4. hot dog/hot dogs

5. spaghetti

6. curry

7. iced tea

8. lemonade

B. Point and say the words.

C. Listen and point.

D. Write the words.
(See pages 63–66.)

3
4
1
2
5
6
8
7

Practice Time

A. Listen and repeat.

What are you **What's he** **What are they**	**going to have?**	**I'm** **He's** **They're**	**going to have**	**a hot dog.** **some curry.**

B. Listen and repeat. Then practice with a partner.

1. you?
burrito

2. he?
spaghetti

3. they?
iced tea

4. you?
french fries

5. he?
taco

6. you?
lemonade

C. Look at page 20. Point to the picture and practice with a partner.

D. Listen and sing along. (See "What Are You Going to Have?" on page 59.)

Phonics Time

A. Listen and repeat.

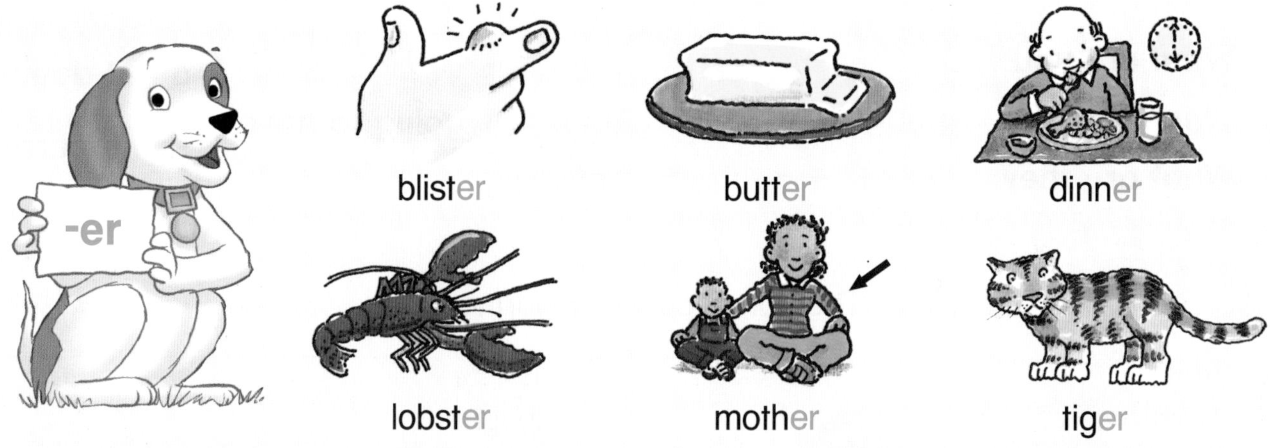
-er
blister
butter
dinner
lobster
mother
tiger

B. Listen and circle.

1.	2.	3.	4.
sister	brother	bigger	Peter
swimmer	Buster	blister	mother

C. Read the sentences. Write the numbers. Then listen.

1. Buster the tiger had a blister.
2. Mother gave Buster lobster for dinner.
3. "I like lobster," said Buster.
4. Buster put butter on the blister.
5. But the blister got bigger.

6

During the Year

Conversation Time

A. Listen and repeat.

B. Listen and point to the speakers.

C. Role-play the conversation with two other students.

1.
What's your favorite subject?
I like math. It's fun.

2.
Excuse me. Where's the library?
Go straight. It's across from the music room.

3.
Thanks.
Sure.

4.
Oh. It's time for art class.
Great. That's my favorite.

D. Review. Listen and repeat.

16
2x5=

 I put away the books.

And I swept the floor.

 Thank you very much!

Word Time

A. Listen and repeat.

1. spring
2. summer
3. fall
4. winter
5. plant flowers
6. pick apples
7. build a snowman
8. go to the beach
9. play in the leaves
10. go skiing

B. Point and say the words.

C. Listen and point.

D. Write the words.
(See pages 63–66.)

1
2
3
4
9
6
10
7
8

Practice Time

A. Listen and repeat.

I'll plant flowers in the spring.

I'll = I will	You'll = You will
He'll = He will	She'll = She will
We'll = We will	They'll = They will

I won't go skiing.

won't = will not

B. Listen and repeat. Then practice with a partner.

1. I / go to the beach / summer
   pick apples

2. You / pick apples / fall
   go to the beach

3. They / build a snowman / winter
   plant flowers

4. He / plant flowers / spring
   build a snowman

5. We / play in the leaves / fall
   go skiing

6. She / go skiing / winter
   play in the leaves

C. Look at page 24. Point to the picture and practice with a partner.

D. Listen and sing along. (See "He'll Pick Apples in the Fall" on page 59.)

Phonics Time

A. Listen and repeat.

al
au
aw
fall
laundry
crawl
talk
saucer
draw

B. Listen and circle.

1.	2.	3.	4.	5.
small	claw	paw	call	walk
shawl	tall	wall	chalk	jaw

C. Read the sentences. Write the numbers. Then listen.

1. Paul isn't tall. He's small.
2. Paul can't talk. He can't walk. He can't do the laundry.
3. But Paul can crawl. Oh, no! Paul is in the hall.
4. Paul has chalk. Look at the wall. He can draw.

Review 2

Story Time

Digger's World

A. Listen and repeat.

1.
Excuse me. I'm looking for the music room.
Go straight. It's on the left.

2.
I'm going to see a show. What are you going to do?
I'm going to buy a donut.

3.
Excuse me. What are you eating?
Curry. Try some. It's delicious.
Mm. It's good!

4.
What are you going to have?
I'm going to have some curry, some french fries, a taco, a burrito, and some lemonade.

5.
Hey, Digger!
Hi, Max. It's time for the show.

6.
Try some, Digger. It's curry. It's good.
No, thanks.
Sh! Be quiet!

B. Look at **A**. Listen and point.

C. Listen. Circle True or False.

1. True False **2.** True False **3.** True False **4.** True False **5.** True False

D. Role-play these scenes.

Activity Time

A. Listen and write.

1. P____l is going to t____k to a tig____.
2. Pet____ is going to dr____ a bott____.
3. The lobst____ is going to cr____l in the pudd____.
4. My moth____ is going to make dinn____ for my unc____.

Paul
Peter

B. Complete the puzzle. What's Annie going to have?

1. He'll plant flowers in the ____________.
2. I'm going to rent a ____________. I'm not going to see a show.
3. She's hungry. She's going to buy a ____________.
4. What's he going to have? He's going to have a ____________.
5. We'll play in the leaves in the ____________.
6. They'll go to the beach in the ____________.
7. I'll go skiing in the ____________.
8. I'm going to mail a ____________.

I'm going to have some ____________.
f
1.
2.
3.
4.
h
5.
6.
7.
8.
s

At the Aquarium

Conversation Time

A. Listen and repeat.

B. Listen and point to the speakers.

C. Role-play the conversation with a partner.

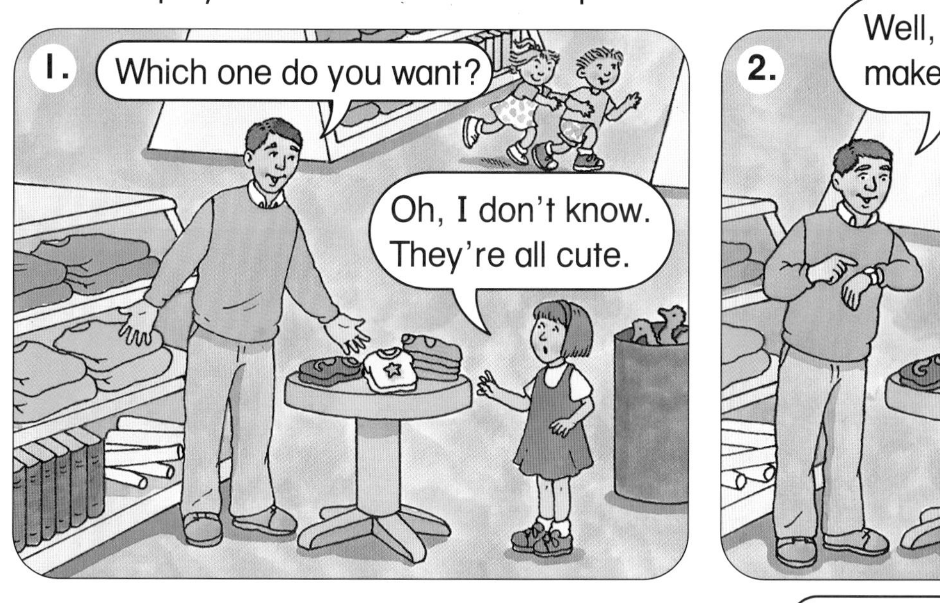

1.
Which one do you want?
Oh, I don't know. They're all cute.

2.
Well, it's time to go. Please make up your mind.
Um, okay. I'll take this one.

3.
Are you sure?
I'm positive.

4.
Great. Let's get it.
Dad, the cashier is over here.

D. Review. Listen and repeat.

Excuse me. I'm looking for the bathroom. Is it far?

Not really. Go straight. It's on the left.

Thanks.

No problem.

Word Time

A. Listen and repeat.

1. whale
2. dolphin
3. eel
4. shark
5. octopus
6. crab
7. big
8. small
9. fast
10. slow

B. Point and say the words.

C. Listen and point.

D. Write the words.
(See pages 63–66.)

1
9
2
10
4
5
6
3
7
8

Practice Time

A. Listen and repeat.

The whale is bigger than the dolphin.

big → bigger		small → smaller	
fast → faster		slow → slower	

B. Listen and repeat. Then practice with a partner.

1. crab/slow/dolphin

2. shark/small/whale

3. whale/big/eel

4. octopus/big/crab

5. eel/small/shark

6. dolphin/fast/octopus

C. Look at page 30. Point to the picture and practice with a partner.

D. Listen and chant. (See "The Whale Is Bigger Than the Dolphin" on page 60.)

Phonics Time

A. Listen and repeat.

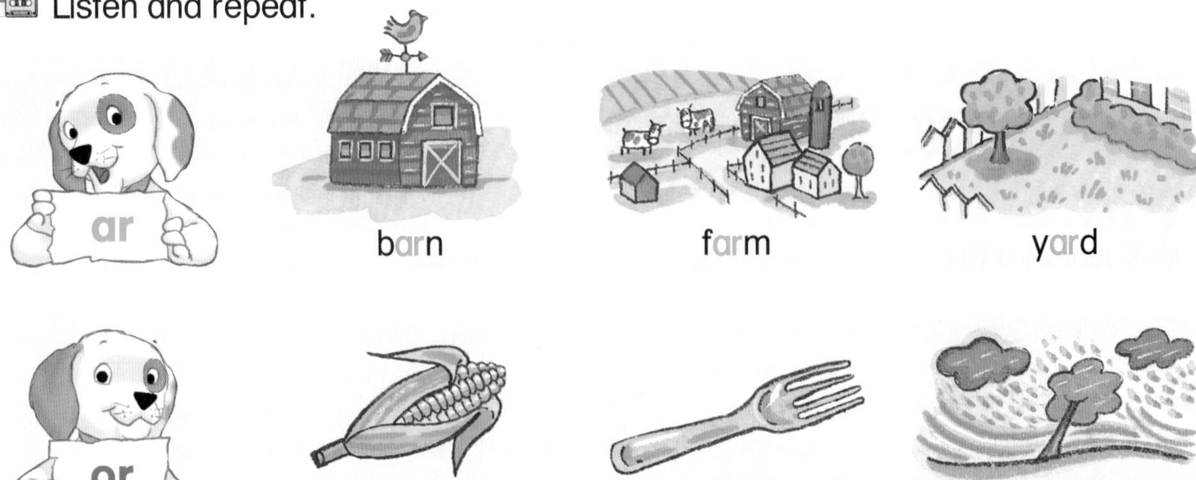
ar
barn
farm
yard
or
corn
fork
storm

B. Does it have ar or or? Listen and circle.

1. ar or 2. ar or 3. ar or 4. ar or 5. ar or 6. ar or

C. Read the sentences. Write the numbers. Then listen.

1. Bart had a farm. One day there was a storm.
2. The sky was dark, but Bart was smart.
   He put the corn in the barn.
3. But the wind blew very hard.
4. Look at the corn in the yard!

8

At the Safari Park

Conversation Time

A. Listen and repeat.

B. Listen and point to the speakers.

C. Role-play the conversation with two other students.

1.
Dad! Guess what!
What?

2.
There's a monkey on the car!
Quick! Shut the window.

3.
Look! There it is.
Oh, it's cute.

4.
It's not cute. It's scary.
Don't worry. It won't hurt you.
Aw! It's going away.

D. Review. Listen and repeat.

 I'm going to take a picture.

 Be very careful!

 Oh, no!

I told you to be careful.

Word Time

A. Listen and repeat.

1. elephant
2. cheetah
3. giraffe
4. snake
5. turtle
6. chimpanzee
7. tall
8. short
9. fat
10. thin

B. Point and say the words.

C. Listen and point.

D. Write the words.
(See pages 63–66.)

1
2
3
4
5
6
7
8
9
10

Practice Time

A. Listen and repeat.

Which one is the tallest? **The giraffe is the tallest.**

tall	→	tallest	short	→	shortest
fat	→	fattest	thin	→	thinnest
fast	→	fastest	slow	→	slowest

B. Listen and repeat. Then practice with a partner.

1. short? chimpanzee

2. tall? giraffe

3. fat? elephant

4. slow? turtle

5. fast? cheetah

6. thin? snake

C. Look at page 34. Point to the picture and practice with a partner.

D. Listen and sing along. (See "Which One Is the Tallest?" on page 60.)

Phonics Time

A. Listen and repeat.

ou
house
mouse
mouth
ow
brown
gown
town

B. Do they both have the same vowel sound? Listen and circle ✔ or ✘.

1.	2.	3.	4.	5.	6.
cloud	cow	out	couch	clown	down
mouse	snow	owl	home	tow	shout
✔ ✘	✔ ✘	✔ ✘	✔ ✘	✔ ✘	✔ ✘

C. Read the sentences. Write the numbers. Then listen.

1. A silly little mouse lived in a big house.
2. She went to town in an evening gown.
3. She met a brown trout and started to shout.
4. "Please don't shout, little mouse," said the trout.

9

By the Seashore

Conversation Time

A. Listen and repeat.

B. Listen and point to the speakers.

C. Role-play the conversation with three other students.

1.
Oh! I missed the ball.
We won! We won!

2.
Congratulations.
Nice game. It was close.
Yeah, it was.

3.
Do you want to play again?
Sure.

4.
This time we'll win.
We'll see.

D. Review. Listen and repeat.

 Guess what!

 What?

 There's a fish on your head!

 Oh, no!

 Don't worry. It's cute. It won't hurt you.

Word Time

A. Listen and repeat.

1. play Ping-Pong
2. play badminton
3. snorkel
4. go fishing
5. go horseback riding
6. go sailing
7. in-line skate
8. listen to music

B. Point and say the words.

C. Listen and point.

D. Write the words.
(See pages 63–66.)

2
4
6
8
3
7
5
1

Practice Time

A. Listen and repeat.

What	do you does he	like to do?

I like He likes	to listen to music.

B. Listen and repeat. Then practice with a partner.

1. she?
go fishing

2. they?
go sailing

3. you?
snorkel

4. you?
play badminton

5. he?
in-line skate

6. they?
play Ping-Pong

C. Look at page 38. Point to the picture and practice with a partner.

D. Listen and chant. (See "What Do You Like to Do?" on page 61.)

Phonics Time

A. Listen and repeat.

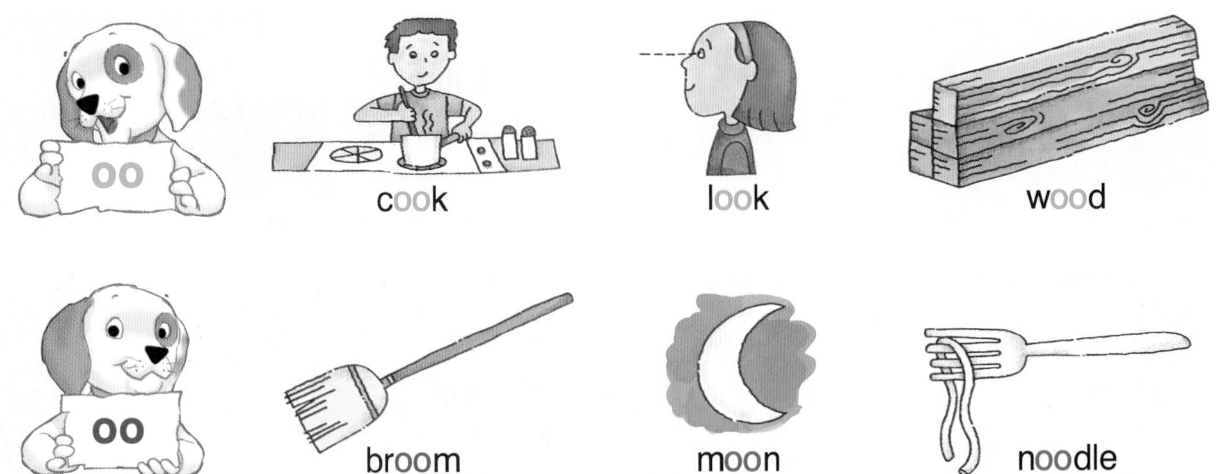
oo
cook
look
wood
oo
broom
moon
noodle

B. Which word has a different **oo** sound? Listen and circle.

1.	2.	3.	4.	5.
book	kangaroo	moose	scooter	rooster
boot	moon	school	hook	took
cook	foot	hood	zoo	wood

C. Read the sentences. Write the numbers. Then listen.

1. Ms. Hood and her poodle went to the zoo.
2. They saw a red rooster and a kangaroo.
3. They looked at a moose, and they looked at the moon.
4. And then they went to school on a scooter.

ZOO

Review 3

Story Time

Digger's World

A. Listen and repeat.

1.
Let's play a game. There's a dog, a giraffe, and an elephant. Which one is the tallest?
Hmm. I don't know.
ANIMALS

2.
Hurry, Max. Make up your mind.
I know! The giraffe is the tallest.

3.
You're right! Congratulations! Do you want to play again?
Sure! This is fun. I like to play games.

4.
A dog, a whale, and a turtle. Which one is the biggest?
The whale is the biggest. Right?

5.
Right! Do you want to play again?
No, Digger! This time you play. Which dog is the cutest?

6.
I don't know, Max.
Guess what, Digger! You're the cutest!

B. Look at **A**. Listen and point.

C. Listen. Circle True or False.

1. True False **2.** True False **3.** True False **4.** True False **5.** True False

D. Role-play these scenes.

Activity Time

A. Listen and write.

1. 

The __________ and __________ are on the __________.

2. 

The __________ and __________ are in the __________.

3. Can a __________ __________ __________?

B. Read and circle True or False.

1. The whale is bigger than the elephant. True False
2. The chimpanzee is taller than the giraffe. True False
3. The turtle is the shortest. True False

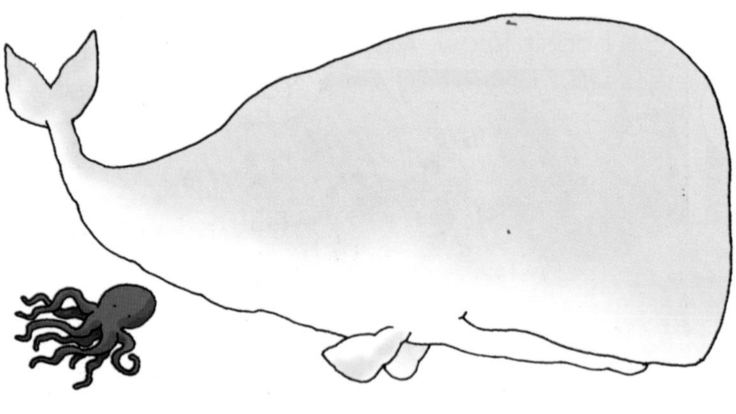

C. What do you like to do? Ask your classmates. Write their names.

__________ likes to play Ping-Pong.

__________ likes to go fishing.

__________ likes to in-line skate.

__________ likes to listen to music.

__________ likes to snorkel.

__________ likes to play badminton.

10

At Summer Camp

Conversation Time

A. Listen and repeat.

B. Listen and point to the speakers.

C. Role-play the conversation with a partner.

1.
Wow! What a cool kite!
Thanks. I made it myself.

2.
You're kidding!
No, it's true. I made it.

3.
Was it hard?
No, it was easy. I'll show you.

4.
Great! What do we need?
Paper and string. Let's get some.

D. Review. Listen and repeat.

What do you like to do?

I like to play Ping-Pong.

Do you want to play?

Sure.

Word Time

A. Listen and repeat.

1. collect stickers
2. sing
3. build a model
4. take a nap
5. read a comic book
6. make a video
7. paint
8. cycle

B. Point and say the words.

C. Listen and point.

D. Write the words.
(See pages 63–66.)

50
22
2
6
8
7
3
1
5
4

Practice Time

A. Listen and repeat.

We like She likes	singing, but	we don't she doesn't	like building models.

build a model → building models

collect → collecting	sing → singing	build → building	take → taking
read → reading	make → making	paint → painting	cycle → cycling

B. Listen and repeat. Then practice with a partner.

1. I/make videos/collect stickers

2. They/collect stickers/make videos

3. She/cycle/take a nap

4. He/take a nap/cycle

ZZZ

5. You/read comic books/paint

6. She/paint/read comic books

C. Look at page 44. Point to the picture and practice with a partner.

D. Listen and chant. (See "I Like Painting" on page 61.)

Phonics Time

A. Listen and repeat.

er
ir
ur
BERT
clerk
bird
curry
dessert
shirt
purse

B. Listen and match.

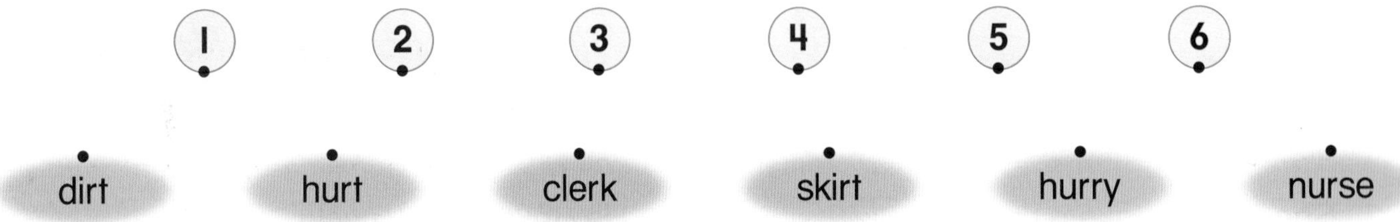
1
2
3
4
5
6
dirt
hurt
clerk
skirt
hurry
nurse

C. Read the sentences. Write the numbers. Then listen.

1. Bert the clerk was in a hurry.
2. He ripped his shirt. He burned the curry.
3. He hurt his foot. He called a nurse.
4. And then he ate a big dessert.

11

At the Planetarium

Conversation Time

A. Listen and repeat.

B. Listen and point to the speakers.

C. Role-play the conversation with two other students.

1.
PLANETARIUM
Wow! Did you see all the planets and stars?
Yeah! That was a great show.

2.
Ms. Apple, can we go to the snack bar?
Can we go to the gift shop?
No, kids. We don't have time.

3.
Aw. But I want to buy a gift for my dad.
And I'm thirsty.
THE MOON

4.
Please, Ms. Apple. We'll hurry.
Sorry, kids. We have to catch the bus.

D. Review. Listen and repeat.

I saw a movie at the museum today.

Did you have lunch at the museum?

No, I didn't. I'm hungry.

Let's have some dinner.

Word Time

A. Listen and repeat.

1. Mercury
2. Venus
3. Earth
4. Mars
5. Jupiter
6. Saturn
7. Uranus
8. Neptune
9. Pluto

B. Point and say the words.

C. Listen and point.

D. Write the words.
(See pages 63–66.)

1
2
3
4
5
6
7
8
9
PLANETARIUM

Practice Time

A. Listen and repeat.

I want He wants	to see Mercury. Let	me him	look.

I → me he → him she → her
we → us they → them

B. Listen and repeat. Then practice with a partner.

1. She/Mars

2. They/Saturn

3. I/Jupiter

4. He/Neptune

5. We/Venus

6. She/Pluto

C. Look at page 48. Point to the picture and practice with a partner.

D. Listen and sing along. (See "I Want to See Mercury" on page 62.)

Phonics Time

A. Listen and repeat.

oi
boil
oil
point
oy
boy
joy
oyster

B. Do they both have the same vowel sound? Listen and write ✔ or ✘.

1. Roy / boil ☐
2. join / joy ☐
3. nose / toy ☐
4. soy / son ☐
5. frown / boys ☐

C. Read the sentences. Write the numbers. Then listen.

1. Roy and the boy loved oysters. They loved them boiled.
2. They loved them broiled.
3. They loved them cooked in oil.
4. They put them in foil.
5. And jumped and jumped for joy!

OIL

12 At School

Conversation Time

A. Listen and repeat.

B. Listen and point to the speakers.

C. Role-play the conversation with a partner.

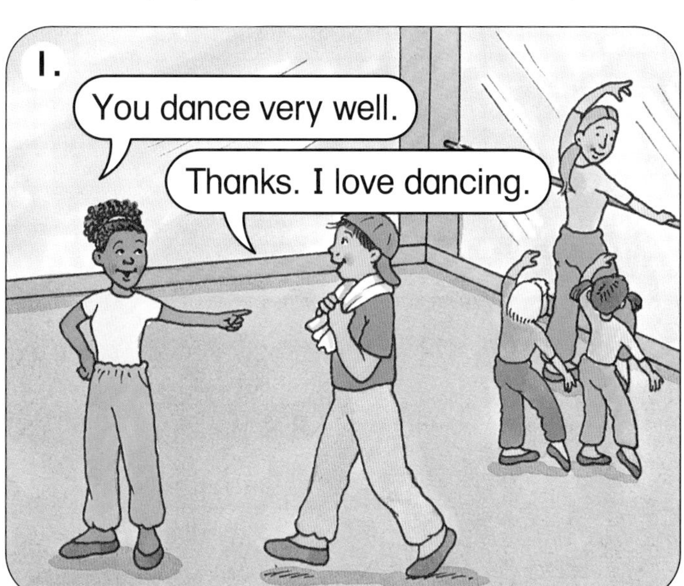
1.
You dance very well.
Thanks. I love dancing.

2.

I don't dance very well.

Sure you do. You're a good dancer.

3.
But I don't practice enough.
Well, practice makes perfect.

4.
I have an idea. Let's practice together.
That's a great idea. Thanks.

D. Review. Listen and repeat.

7×7=

What's your favorite subject?

I like art. Look at my kite.

That's great. Did you make it?

Yes, I did. It was easy.

Word Time

A. Listen and repeat.

1.	musician	**2.**	play the violin
3.	engineer	**4.**	build things
5.	vet	**6.**	help animals
7.	computer programmer	**8.**	program computers
9.	nurse	**10.**	take care of people
11.	artist	**12.**	draw

B. Point and say the words.

C. Listen and point.

D. Write the words.
(See pages 63–66.)

4
3
5
7
8
6
2
1
10
9
12
11

Practice Time

A. Listen and repeat.

Why	do you does she	want to be a vet?	Because	I like she likes	helping animals.

play → playing build → building help → helping
program → programming take → taking draw → drawing

B. Listen and repeat. Then practice with a partner.

1. you/engineer?
build things

2. he/computer programmer?
program computers

3. she/vet?
help animals

4. he/nurse?
take care of people

5. you/artist?
draw

6. she/musician?
play the violin

C. Look at page 52. Point to the picture and practice with a partner.

D. Listen and sing along. (See "Why Do You Want to Be a Vet?" on page 62.)

Phonics Time

A. Listen and repeat.

Review
marker
walk
saucer
draw
park
fork
cloud
shower
cook
spoon
clerk
shirt
purse
coin
boy

B. Listen and circle.

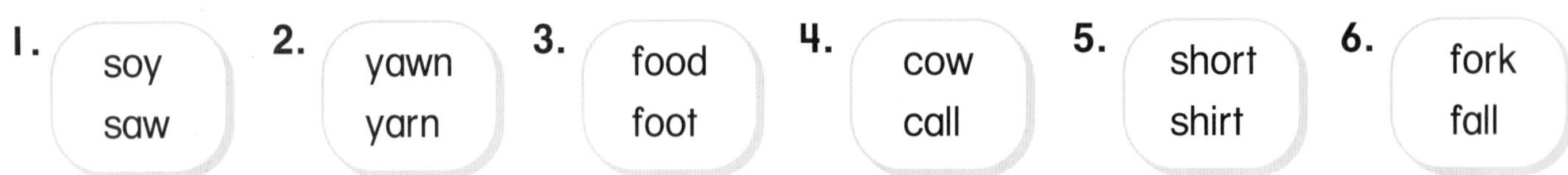
1. soy saw
2. yawn yarn
3. food foot
4. cow call
5. short shirt
6. fork fall

C. Read the sentences. Write the numbers. Then listen.

1. Did you see the tall, thin clerk?
   She walked into a big blue shirt.
2. Paul has a saucer, a fork, and a spoon.
   He eats noodles on the moon.
3. Look at the yellow and black basketball.
   Do you like to play in the yard in the fall?

PAUL

Review 4

Story Time

Digger's World

A. Listen and repeat.

1.
What a cool cookie, Digger!
Thanks, Max. I made it myself.

2.
You're kidding. Was it hard?
No, it was easy. I love baking.

3.
I like baking, too. But I don't bake well.
Sure you do. I have an idea. Let's bake together.

4.
Great! Let's bake a big cake together. What do we need?
I'll show you.

5.
Later...
That wasn't hard. It was easy. This cake is great.
Well, practice makes perfect.

6.
Wow! That was a great cake.
Can we make donuts now?
Oh, Max!
See you in Level 5!

B. Look at **A**. Listen and point.

C. Listen. Circle True or False.

1. True False **2.** True False **3.** True False **4.** True False **5.** True False

D. Role-play these scenes.

Activity Time

A. Listen and write.

1.

2.

3.

B. Read and match.

1. Why do you want to be an engineer? •	• Because I like helping animals.
2. Why do you want to be a vet? •	• Because I like playing the violin.
3. Why do you want to be a musician? •	• Because I like drawing.
4. Why do you want to be an artist? •	• Because I like building things.

C. Listen and circle **a** or **b**.

1.
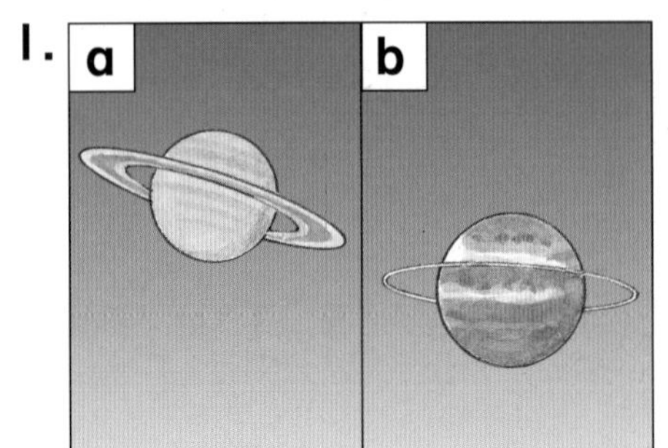
a
b

2.

a
b

3.

a
b

Songs and Chants

1 Did Ted Watch the Sunrise?

(Melody: The Bridge of Avignon)

Did Ted watch the sunrise?
No, he didn't. No, he didn't.
Did Ted watch the sunrise?
No, he didn't. He played cards.

Did Bill climb a mountain?
No, he didn't. No, he didn't.
Did Bill climb a mountain?
No, he didn't. He played cards.

Did Joe clean the tent?
Yes, he did. Yes, he did.
Did Joe clean the tent?
Yes, he did. He cleaned the tent.

2 Dan and Penny Saw a Show

(Melody: Mary Had a Little Lamb)

Dan and Penny saw a show, saw a show,
saw a show.
Dan and Penny saw a show.
They didn't win a prize.

Bob and Annie won a prize, won a prize,
won a prize.
Bob and Annie won a prize.
They didn't buy tickets.

Bill and Ivy bought tickets, bought tickets,
bought tickets.
Bill and Ivy bought tickets.
They didn't see a show.

3 What Did You Do?

(Melody: For He's a Jolly Good Fellow)

What did you do?
What did you do?
What did you do?
We made the bed.

What did she do?
What did she do?
What did she do?
She set the table.

What did he do?
What did he do?
What did he do?
He swept the floor.

What did they do?
What did they do?
What did they do?
They did the laundry.

4 I'm Going to Rent a Video

(Melody: Good Night, Ladies)

I'm going to rent a video.
He's going to rent a video.
We're going to rent a video.
We aren't going to mail a letter.

He's going to visit a friend.
She's going to visit a friend.
They're going to visit a friend.
They aren't going to ride the bus.

I'm going to buy a donut.
He's going to buy a donut.
We're going to buy a donut.
We aren't going to see a movie.

5 What Are You Going to Have?

(Melody: The Farmer in the Dell)

MENU
MENU

What are you going to have?
What are you going to have?
What are you going to have?
We're going to have some tacos.

What's she going to have?
What's she going to have?
What's she going to have?
She's going to have a burrito.

What's he going to have?
What's he going to have?
What's he going to have?
He's going to have some curry.

What are they going to have?
What are they going to have?
What are they going to have?
They're going to have some french fries.

6 He'll Pick Apples in the Fall

(Melody: She'll Be Coming 'Round the Mountain)

He'll pick apples in the fall, in the fall.
He'll pick apples in the fall, in the fall.
He won't build a snowman.
He won't build a snowman.
He'll pick apples in the fall.

She'll plant flowers in the spring, in the spring.
She'll plant flowers in the spring, in the spring.
She won't play in the leaves.
She won't play in the leaves.
She'll plant flowers in the spring.

7 The Whale Is Bigger Than the Dolphin

The whale is bigger than the dolphin.
The dolphin is smaller than the whale.
The octopus is faster than the crab.
The crab is slower than the octopus.

The dolphin is bigger than the octopus.
The octopus is smaller than the dolphin.
The shark is faster than the eel.
The eel is slower than the shark.

8 Which One Is the Tallest?

(Melody: Did You Ever See a Lassie?)

Which one is the tallest, the tallest, the tallest?
Which one is the tallest, the tallest you see?
The giraffe is the tallest, the tallest, the tallest.
The giraffe is the tallest, the tallest I see.

Which one is the shortest, the shortest, the shortest?
Which one is the shortest, the shortest you see?
The turtle is the shortest, the shortest, the shortest.
The turtle is the shortest, the shortest I see.

Which one is the thinnest, the thinnest, the thinnest?
Which one is the thinnest, the thinnest you see?
The snake is the thinnest, the thinnest, the thinnest.
The snake is the thinnest, the thinnest I see.

9 What Do You Like to Do?

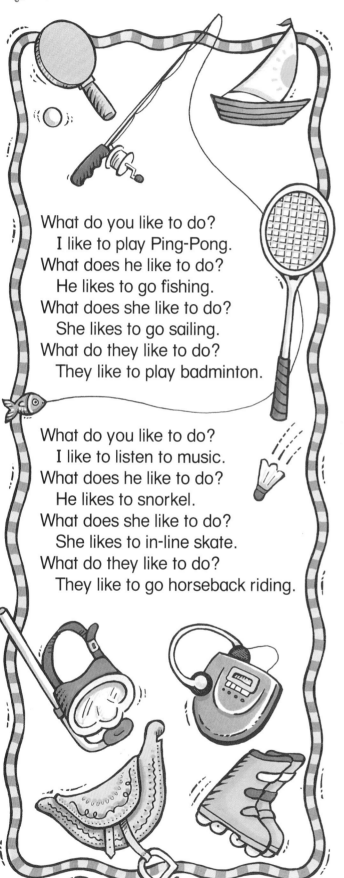

What do you like to do?
I like to play Ping-Pong.
What does he like to do?
He likes to go fishing.
What does she like to do?
She likes to go sailing.
What do they like to do?
They like to play badminton.

What do you like to do?
I like to listen to music.
What does he like to do?
He likes to snorkel.
What does she like to do?
She likes to in-line skate.
What do they like to do?
They like to go horseback riding.

10 I Like Painting

I like painting,
but I don't like making videos.
She likes making videos,
but she doesn't like painting.

I like singing,
but I don't like building models.
He likes building models,
but he doesn't like singing.

I like collecting stickers,
but I don't like taking naps.
They like taking naps,
but they don't like collecting stickers.

We like cycling,
but we don't like reading comic books.
They like reading comic books,
but they don't like cycling.

11 I Want to See Mercury

(Melody: When Johnny Comes Marching Home)

I want to see Mercury.
Hurrah, hurrah!
I want to see Mercury.
Hurrah, hurrah!
I want to see Mercury.
I want to see Mercury.
Let me look. Let me look.
Please let me look.

She wants to see Jupiter.
Hurrah, hurrah!
She wants to see Jupiter.
Hurrah, hurrah!
She wants to see Jupiter.
She wants to see Jupiter.
Let her look. Let her look.
Please let her look.

He wants to see Saturn.
Hurrah, hurrah!
He wants to see Saturn.
Hurrah, hurrah!
He wants to see Saturn.
He wants to see Saturn.
Let him look. Let him look.
Please let him look.

12 Why Do You Want to Be a Vet?

(Melody: When the Saints Go Marching In)

Why do you want to be a vet?
Why do you want to be a vet?
Because I like helping animals.
Oh, yes, I want to be a vet.

Why does he want to be a programmer?
Why does he want to be a programmer?
Because he likes programming computers.
Oh, yes, he wants to be a programmer.

Why does she want to be a nurse?
Why does she want to be a nurse?
Because she likes taking care of people.
Oh, yes, she wants to be a nurse.

My Picture Dictionary

Write the words.

A a

B b

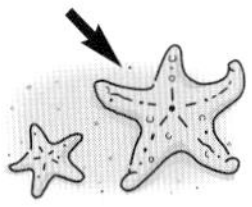

C c

D d

E e

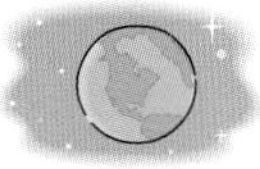

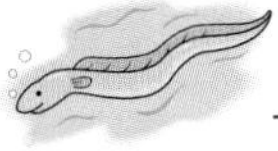

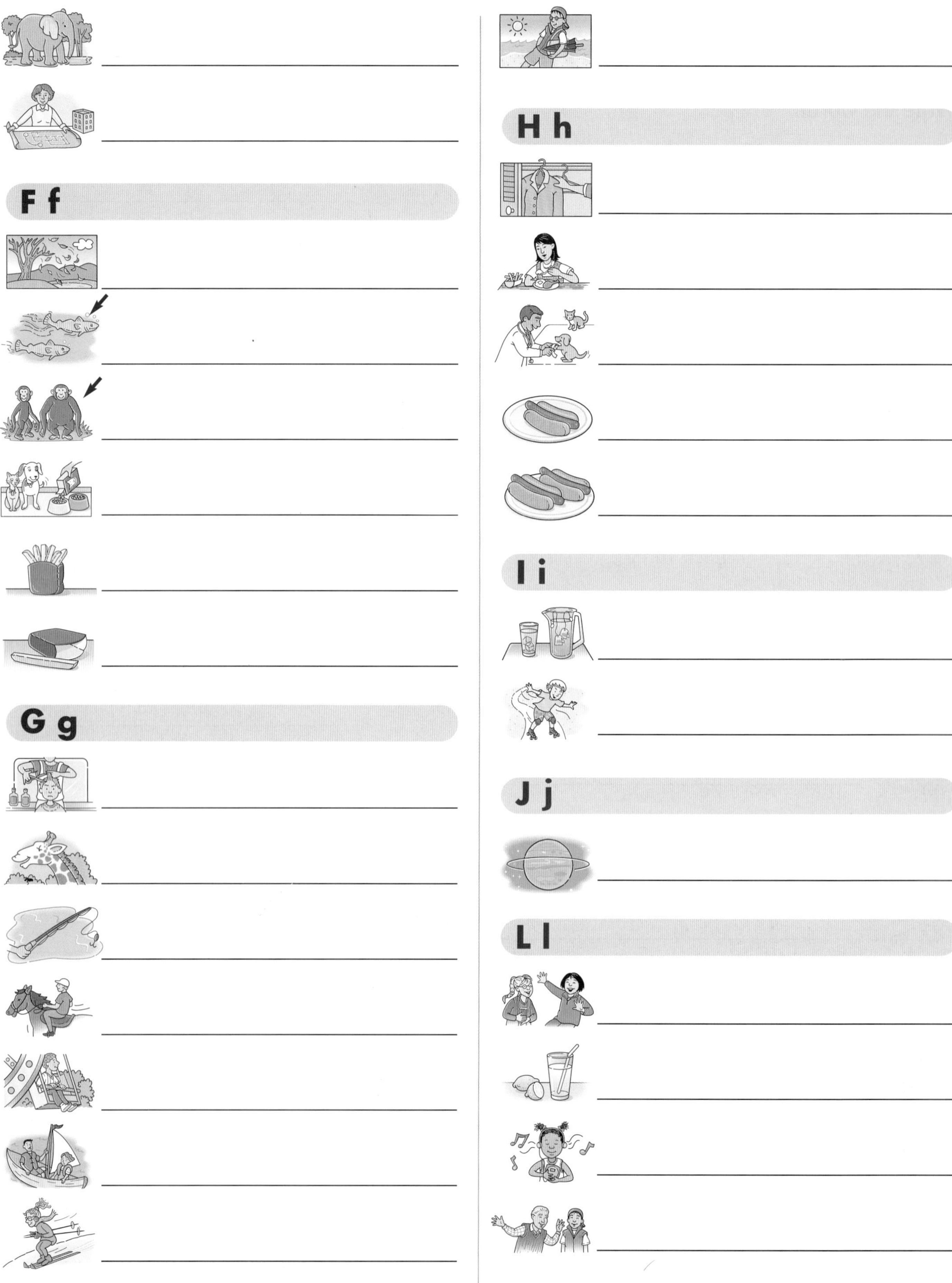

F f
G g
H h
I i
J j
L l

M m

N n

O o

P p

R r

S s

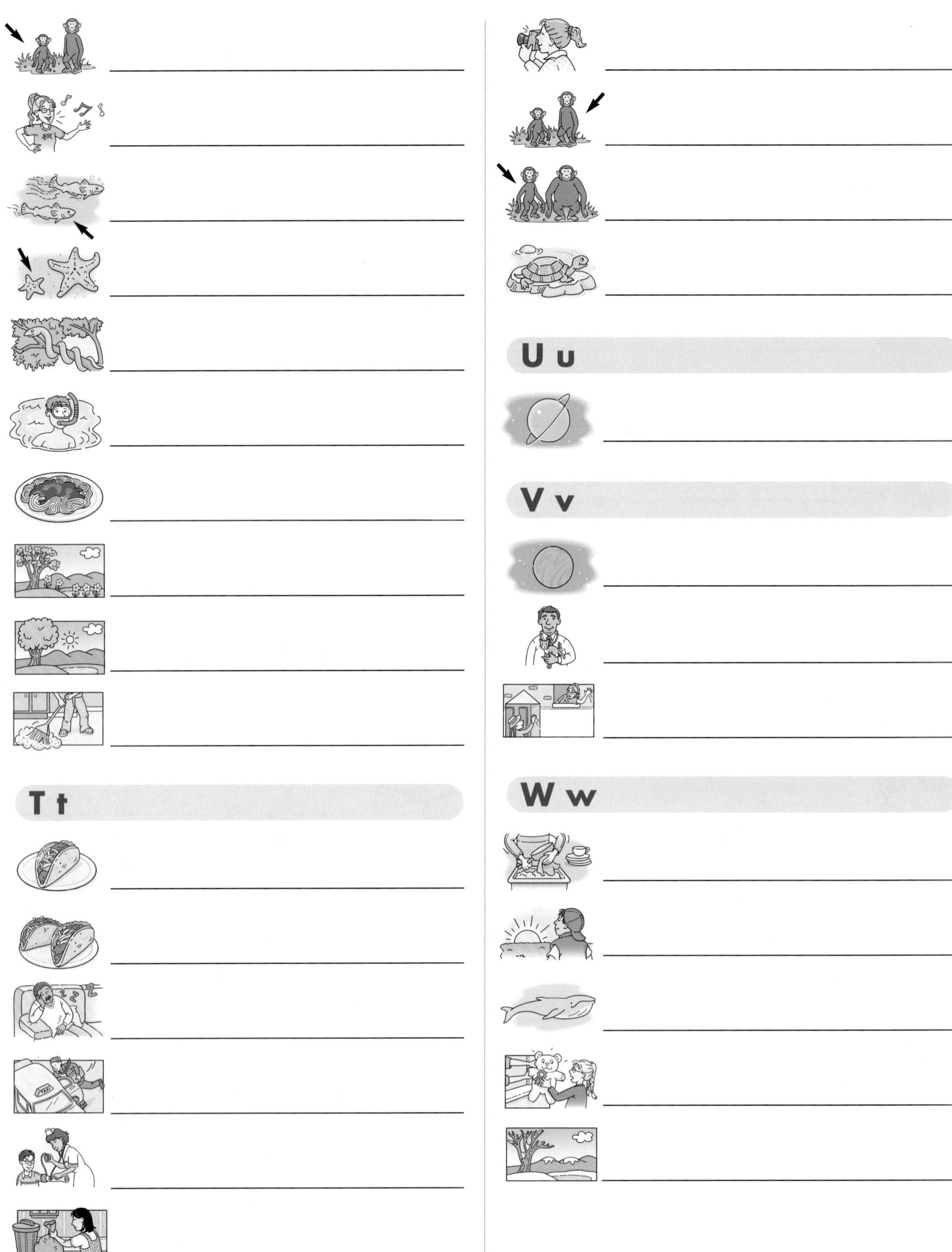
T t
U u
V v
W w
TAXI

☑ Checklist 1 (Units 1–3)

A. I can say these patterns. ☐

1. 

Did you laugh at jokes?
No, I didn't. I listened to stories.

Did they play cards?
Yes, they did.

2. 

She ate cotton candy. She didn't have lunch.

He drank soda pop. He didn't take pictures.

3. 

What did he do?
He took out the garbage.

What did she do?
She fed the pets.

B. I can talk about this picture. ☐

C. I can read these words. ☐

1. baked	2. drum	3. waited	4. fish	5. called
6. planted	7. kissed	8. three	9. cleaned	10. plane

☑ Checklist 2 (Units 4–6)

A. I can say these patterns. ☐

1.

I'm going to mail a letter.
I'm not going to visit a friend.

They're going to see a movie.
They aren't going to buy a donut.

2.

What's she going to have?
She's going to have a taco.

What are you going to have?
I'm going to have some lemonade.

3.

I'll build a snowman in the winter.
I won't pick apples.

I'll plant flowers in the spring.
I won't play in the leaves.

B. I can talk about this picture. ☐

C. I can read these words. ☐

1. dinner **2.** draw **3.** poodle **4.** talk **5.** laundry

6. bottle **7.** fall **8.** uncle **9.** crawl **10.** tiger

☑ Checklist 3 (Units 7–9)

A. I can say these patterns. ☐

1.

The whale is bigger than the shark.

The dolphin is faster than the octopus.

2.

Which one is the tallest?
The giraffe is the tallest.

Which one is the thinnest?
The cheetah is the thinnest.

3.

What do you like to do?
We like to play badminton.

What does she like to do?
She likes to listen to music.

B. I can talk about this picture. ☐

C. I can read these words. ☐

1. fork	**2.** town	**3.** wood	**4.** farm	**5.** mouse
6. look	**7.** yard	**8.** mouth	**9.** moon	**10.** corn

☑ Checklist 4 (Units 10–12)

A. I can say these patterns. ☐

1\. 

I like collecting stickers, but I don't like singing.

She likes reading comic books, but she doesn't like cycling.

2\. 

I want to see Saturn. Let me look.

He wants to see Mars. Let him look.

3\. 

Why do you want to be a vet?
Because I like helping animals.

Why does she want to be a musician?
Because she likes playing the violin.

B. I can talk about this picture. ☐

C. I can read these words. ☐

1. curry	**2.** shirt	**3.** oyster	**4.** spoon	**5.** dessert
6. boil	**7.** marker	**8.** joy	**9.** purse	**10.** point

Word List

The numbers to the right of the entries indicate the page(s) on which the word is introduced. Words in blue appear only in the art (on the Conversation Time pages).

M

N

O

P

R

S

T

U

V

W

Y

Z